Introduction

Welcome to "Credit Repair: A Step-by-Step Guide to Improving Your Credit Score"! If you're reading this book, it's likely that you have some concerns about your credit score and are looking for ways to improve it. Maybe you have a low credit score and are having trouble getting approved for loans or credit cards. Maybe you have a good credit score but want to make it even better so you can qualify for the best interest rates and terms. Whatever your reason for seeking credit repair, this book is here to help.

In the pages that follow, you'll learn about the factors that influence your credit score, how to check and understand your credit report, and what you can do to repair any damage and improve your credit score. You'll also find tips on how to maintain a good credit score and avoid common mistakes that can harm your credit.

By following the advice in this book, you can take control of your credit and set yourself up for financial success. So let's get started on your credit repair journey!

What Is A Credit Score

Your credit score is a numerical representation of your creditworthiness, or how likely you are to repay a loan or credit card debt. It is used by lenders, landlords, and others to evaluate your financial history and make decisions about whether to lend to you or provide you with other financial services. There are several factors that go into determining your credit score, including:

1. **Payment history**: This is the most important factor in determining your credit score. It includes whether you have made your payments on time, and if you have any late payments or collections on your credit report.
2. **Credit utilization**: This is the amount of credit you are using compared to the amount of credit you have available. It is important to keep your credit utilization low, as using a high percentage of your available credit can signal to lenders that you may be overextending yourself financially.
3. **Credit age**: Credit age, also known as credit history length, refers to the length of time you have had credit accounts and how long you have been using credit. Credit age is an important factor in your credit score because it shows lenders and creditors how long you have been using credit and how well you have managed your credit over time.
4. **Total accounts**: Having a mix of different types of credit (such as a mortgage, a car loan, and a credit card) can be a positive factor in determining your credit score. This is because banks and lenders see you are responsible with handling multiple accounts. The more accounts, the better.
5. **Derogatory marks**: Derogatory marks are negative items that can appear on your credit report and have a negative impact on your credit score. Examples of derogatory marks include late payments, collections, bankruptcies, foreclosures, and charge-offs.
6. **Hard inquiries**: Hard inquiries are credit checks that are initiated by lenders or creditors when you apply for credit, such as a credit card or loan. Hard inquiries can have a temporary negative impact on your credit score because they signal to lenders and creditors that you are seeking new credit.

To improve your credit score, you should focus on making all of your payments on time, keeping your credit utilization low, and avoiding opening too many new credit accounts at once. It is also a good idea to check your credit report regularly to make sure there are no errors or inaccuracies that could be affecting your score. If you find any errors, you can dispute them with the credit bureau to have them corrected. Finally, consider seeking the advice of a financial advisor or credit counselor if you are having difficulty managing your debts or improving your credit score.

Payment History

Maintaining a good payment history is crucial for your credit score, and it can have numerous benefits in your personal and financial life. Your payment history accounts for about 35% of your credit score, so it's important to prioritize paying your bills on time to avoid damaging your credit. Here, we'll explore the importance and benefits of maintaining a good payment history, as well as some tips for doing so.

First, let's define what we mean by "payment history." Payment history refers to how consistently you pay your bills on time. This includes credit card bills, mortgage payments, car loans, utility bills, and any other debts you may have. When you pay your bills on time, it shows lenders and creditors that you are reliable and responsible with your finances. On the other hand, if you consistently miss payments or pay your bills late, it can harm your credit score and make it more difficult to get approved for loans or credit cards in the future.

So, why is maintaining a good payment history so important? Here are a few reasons:

1. **It can improve your credit score**: As mentioned, your payment history is a major factor in your credit score. Paying your bills on time can help improve your credit score over time, while late or missed payments can have a negative impact. A good credit score can open doors to better interest rates and loan terms, as well as make it easier to get approved for credit cards and loans.
2. **It can save you money**: A good credit score can mean lower interest rates on loans and credit cards, which can save you hundreds or even thousands of dollars in the long run. For example, if you have a good credit score and get approved for a mortgage with a 3% interest rate, you'll pay significantly less in interest over the life of the loan than if you had a lower credit score and qualified for a mortgage with a 5% interest rate.
3. **It can give you financial flexibility**: Having a good credit score can give you more financial flexibility and options. If you need to borrow money in the future, you'll have a better chance of getting approved for loans and credit cards with favorable terms. You may also be able

to qualify for higher credit limits, which can be helpful if you need to make a large purchase or have an emergency expense.

Now that we've discussed the importance and benefits of maintaining a good payment history, let's go over some tips for doing so:

1. **Set up payment reminders**: One easy way to ensure that you never miss a payment is to set up payment reminders. You can do this through your bank or credit card issuer, or you can use a personal finance app or calendar to set reminders for yourself.
2. **Automate your payments**: Another option is to automate your payments by setting up automatic debits from your bank account. This way, you won't have to remember to pay your bills manually each month, and you can be confident that your payments will be made on time.
3. **Pay more than the minimum payment**: If you have credit card debt, it's a good idea to pay more than the minimum payment each month. This will help you pay off your debt faster and reduce the amount of interest you pay.
4. **Use a budget**: Creating and sticking to a budget can help you keep track of your expenses and ensure that you have enough money to pay your bills on time. If you have trouble budgeting, consider using a personal finance app or seeking the help of a financial planner.
5. **Don't take on more debt than you can handle**: It's important to be realistic about how much debt you can handle. If you're already struggling to make your monthly payments, taking on more debt may only make matters worse. Be mindful of your financial limits and only borrow what you can afford to pay back.
6. **Don't close old credit accounts**: If you have credit accounts that you no longer use, it may be tempting to close them to declutter your financial life. However, closing old credit accounts can actually harm your credit score because it reduces your overall credit limit and can lower your credit utilization ratio. If you don't want to use the account, simply leave it open and don't use it.
7. **Check your credit report regularly**: It's a good idea to check your credit report regularly to make sure there are no errors or fraudulent activity that could be affecting your payment history. You can request a free copy of your credit report from each of the three major credit bureaus (Equifax, Experian, and TransUnion) once a year.

In conclusion, maintaining a good payment history is essential for your credit score and overall financial health. By paying your bills on time, you can improve your credit score, save money on interest, and have more financial flexibility. By following the tips outlined above, you can set yourself up for financial success and avoid the negative consequences of a poor payment history.

Credit Utilization

Maintaining a good credit utilization ratio is important for your credit score, and it can have numerous benefits in your personal and financial life. Your credit utilization ratio, also known as your debt-to-credit ratio, refers to the amount of credit you are using compared to the amount of credit you have available. It is calculated by dividing your total credit card balances by your total credit limits. For example, if you have a total credit limit of $10,000 and a total credit card balance of $2,000, your credit utilization ratio would be 20%. Credit utilization accounts for about 30% of your credit score, so it's important to keep it in check to maintain a good credit score. Here, we'll explore the importance and benefits of maintaining a good credit utilization ratio, as well as some tips for doing so.

First, let's discuss the importance of credit utilization. A high credit utilization ratio can indicate to lenders and creditors that you are relying too heavily on credit, which can be seen as a red flag. It may also suggest that you are struggling to pay off your debts, which can lower your credit score. On the other hand, a low credit utilization ratio can show that you are using credit responsibly and have the ability to pay off your debts. A good credit utilization ratio is generally considered to be below 30%, but the ideal ratio will vary depending on your credit history and other factors.

Now that we've established the importance of credit utilization, let's talk about the benefits of maintaining a good credit utilization ratio:

1. **It can improve your credit score**: As mentioned, your credit utilization ratio is a major factor in your credit score. Keeping your credit utilization ratio low can help improve your credit score over time, while a high credit utilization ratio can have a negative impact. A good credit score can open doors to better interest rates and loan terms, as well as make it easier to get approved for credit cards and loans.
2. **It can save you money**: A good credit score can mean lower interest rates on loans and credit cards, which can save you hundreds or even thousands of dollars in the long run. For example, if you have a good credit score and get approved for a mortgage with a 3% interest rate, you'll pay significantly less in interest over the life of the loan

than if you had a lower credit score and qualified for a mortgage with a 5% interest rate.
3. **It can give you financial flexibility**: Having a good credit score can give you more financial flexibility and options. If you need to borrow money in the future, you'll have a better chance of getting approved for loans and credit cards with favorable terms. You may also be able to qualify for higher credit limits, which can be helpful if you need to make a large purchase or have an emergency expense.

Now that we've discussed the importance and benefits of maintaining a good credit utilization ratio, let's go over some tips for doing so:

1. **Pay off your credit card balances in full each month**: One of the easiest ways to maintain a low credit utilization ratio is to pay off your credit card balances in full each month. This will prevent your balances from accumulating and keep your credit utilization ratio low.
2. **Don't max out your credit cards**: It's a good idea to avoid using more than 30% of your credit limit on any one credit card. For example, if you have a credit card with a $1,000 limit, try not to charge more than $300 on it.
3. **Spread your credit card balances across multiple cards**: If you have multiple credit cards, try to spread your balances across them rather than concentrating all your debt on one card. This can help keep your credit utilization ratio low on each individual card.
4. **Increase your credit limits**: If you have a high credit utilization ratio because you have a low credit limit, consider asking your credit card issuer to increase your credit limit. This can help lower your credit utilization ratio and improve your credit score. Just be careful not to increase your spending along with your credit limit.
5. **Use a balance transfer credit card**: If you have high credit card balances and are paying a lot of interest, you might consider using a balance transfer credit card. These cards allow you to transfer your existing credit card balances to a new card with a lower interest rate. This can help you pay off your debt faster and reduce the amount of interest you pay. Just be aware that balance transfer credit cards often come with fees, so be sure to read the fine print and compare offers before choosing one.
6. **Monitor your credit report and credit utilization ratio regularly**: It's a good idea to check your credit report and credit utilization ratio regularly to make sure there are no errors or fraudulent activity that

could be affecting your credit score. You can request a free copy of your credit report from each of the three major credit bureaus (Equifax, Experian, and TransUnion) once a year. You can also use a personal finance app or credit monitoring service to track your credit utilization ratio.

In conclusion, maintaining a good credit utilization ratio is essential for your credit score and overall financial health. By using credit responsibly and keeping your credit utilization ratio low, you can improve your credit score, save money on interest, and have more financial flexibility. By following the tips outlined above, you can take control of your credit and set yourself up for financial success.

Credit Age

Having a good length of credit history is important for your credit score, and it can have numerous benefits in your personal and financial life. Your credit history refers to the information in your credit report, including your credit accounts, payment history, and credit inquiries. It is used by lenders and creditors to evaluate your creditworthiness and determine your credit score. Credit history accounts for about 15% of your credit score, so it's important to build and maintain a good credit history to maintain a good credit score. Here, we'll explore the importance and benefits of having a good length of credit history, as well as some tips for doing so.

First, let's define what we mean by "good length of credit history." A good length of credit history generally refers to having a credit history that spans several years and includes a variety of credit accounts. This can include credit cards, mortgages, car loans, and other types of credit. Having a long credit history can show lenders and creditors that you have a track record of using credit responsibly and paying your bills on time. On the other hand, having a short credit history or no credit history at all can make it more difficult to get approved for credit cards and loans, and can result in a lower credit score.

Now that we've established the importance of having a good length of credit history, let's talk about the benefits of maintaining a good credit history:

1. **It can improve your credit score**: As mentioned, your credit history is a major factor in your credit score. Having a long credit history with a good payment history can help improve your credit score over time, while a short or poor credit history can have a negative impact. A good credit score can open doors to better interest rates and loan terms, as well as make it easier to get approved for credit cards and loans.
2. **It can save you money**: A good credit score can mean lower interest rates on loans and credit cards, which can save you hundreds or even thousands of dollars in the long run. For example, if you have a good credit score and get approved for a mortgage with a 3% interest rate, you'll pay significantly less in interest over the life of the loan

than if you had a lower credit score and qualified for a mortgage with a 5% interest rate.
3. **It can give you financial flexibility**: Having a good credit score can give you more financial flexibility and options. If you need to borrow money in the future, you'll have a better chance of getting approved for loans and credit cards with favorable terms. You may also be able to qualify for higher credit limits, which can be helpful if you need to make a large purchase or have an emergency expense.

Now that we've discussed the importance and benefits of having a good length of credit history, let's go over some tips for building and maintaining a good credit history:

1. **Get a credit card**: If you don't have any credit history, one of the easiest ways to start building a credit history is to get a credit card. You can start with a secured credit card, which requires a cash collateral deposit, or a student credit card, which is designed for college students with little or no credit history. Just be sure to use your credit card responsibly by paying your bills on time and not exceeding your credit limit.
2. **Use credit responsibly**: To maintain a good credit history, it's important to use credit responsibly. This means paying your bills on time, not overextending yourself with credit, and avoiding high balances on your credit cards.
3. **Don't close old credit accounts**: If you have credit accounts that you no longer use, it may be tempting to close them to declutter your financial life. However, closing old credit accounts can actually harm your credit history because it reduces the length of your credit history and lowers your credit utilization ratio. If you don't want to use the account, simply leave it open and don't use it.
4. **Monitor your credit report regularly**: It's a good idea to check your credit report regularly to make sure there are no errors or fraudulent activity that could be affecting your credit history. You can request a free copy of your credit report from each of the three major credit bureaus (Equifax, Experian, and TransUnion) once a year.
5. **Don't open too many new accounts at once**: While it's important to diversify your credit mix, opening too many new credit accounts in a short period of time can be a red flag to lenders and creditors. It can also lower your credit score temporarily because it increases your credit inquiries, which can be seen as a sign of financial instability.

6. **Use credit responsibly when you're young**: Building a good credit history takes time, so it's important to start using credit responsibly as early as possible. If you're a young adult or college student, consider getting a credit card or taking out a small loan and paying it off on time to start building a good credit history.

In conclusion, having a good length of credit history is essential for your credit score and overall financial health. By using credit responsibly and building a long credit history with a good payment history, you can improve your credit score, save money on interest, and have more financial flexibility. It's important to start building your credit history as early as possible and to be mindful of how you use credit to maintain a good credit history. By following the tips outlined above, you can take control of your credit and set yourself up for financial success in the long term.

Total Credit Accounts

Having multiple credit accounts is important for your credit score, and it can have numerous benefits in your personal and financial life. Having a diverse mix of credit accounts, also known as credit diversity, can show lenders and creditors that you are able to handle different types of credit and are financially responsible. Credit diversity accounts for about 10% of your credit score, so it's important to have multiple credit accounts and use them responsibly to maintain a good credit score. Here, we'll explore the importance and benefits of having multiple credit accounts, as well as some tips for doing so.

First, let's define what we mean by "multiple credit accounts." Multiple credit accounts refer to having a variety of credit accounts, such as credit cards, mortgages, car loans, and other types of credit. Having multiple credit accounts can show lenders and creditors that you are able to handle different types of credit and are financially responsible. On the other hand, having only one or two credit accounts, or no credit accounts at all, can make it more difficult to get approved for credit and loans, and can result in a lower credit score.

Now that we've established the importance of having multiple credit accounts, let's talk about the benefits of maintaining a diverse credit mix:

1. **It can improve your credit score**: As mentioned, having a diverse credit mix is an important factor in your credit score. Having multiple credit accounts with a good payment history can help improve your credit score over time, while having a limited credit mix or poor credit history can have a negative impact. A good credit score can open doors to better interest rates and loan terms, as well as make it easier to get approved for credit cards and loans.
2. **It can save you money**: A good credit score can mean lower interest rates on loans and credit cards, which can save you hundreds or even thousands of dollars in the long run. For example, if you have a good credit score and get approved for a mortgage with a 3% interest rate, you'll pay significantly less in interest over the life of the loan than if you had a lower credit score and qualified for a mortgage with a 5% interest rate.

3. **It can give you financial flexibility**: Having a good credit score can give you more financial flexibility and options. If you need to borrow money in the future, you'll have a better chance of getting approved for loans and credit cards with favorable terms. You may also be able to qualify for higher credit limits, which can be helpful if you need to make a large purchase or have an emergency expense.

Now that we've discussed the importance and benefits of having multiple credit accounts, let's go over some tips for building and maintaining a diverse credit mix:

1. **Get a credit card**: If you don't have any credit accounts, one of the easiest ways to start building a diverse credit mix is to get a credit card. You can start with a secured credit card, which requires a cash collateral deposit, or a student credit card, which is designed for college students with little or no credit history. Just be sure to use your credit card responsibly by paying your bills on time and not exceeding your credit limit.
2. **Use credit responsibly**: To maintain a good credit mix, it's important to use credit responsibly. This means paying your bills on time, not overextending yourself with credit, and avoiding high balances on your credit cards.
3. **Diversify your credit mix**: To build a diverse credit mix, consider getting different types of credit, such as a mortgage, car loan, or personal loan. Just be sure to only take on credit that you can afford to pay back.
4. **Don't open too many new accounts at once**: While it's important to diversify your credit mix, opening too many new credit accounts in a short period of time can be a red flag to lenders and creditors. It can also lower your credit score temporarily because it increases your credit inquiries, which can be seen as a sign of financial instability.
5. **Monitor your credit report regularly**: It's a good idea to check your credit report regularly to make sure there are no errors or fraudulent activity that could be affecting your credit mix. You can request a free copy of your credit report from each of the three major credit bureaus (Equifax, Experian, and TransUnion) once a year.
6. **Use credit responsibly when you're young**: Building a good credit mix takes time, so it's important to start using credit responsibly as early as possible. If you're a young adult or college student, consider

getting a credit card or taking out a small loan and paying it off on time to start building a good credit history.

In conclusion, having multiple credit accounts is essential for your credit score and overall financial health. By using credit responsibly and building a diverse credit mix with a good payment history, you can improve your credit score, save money on interest, and have more financial flexibility. It's important to start building your credit mix as early as possible and to be mindful of how you use credit to maintain a good credit history. By following the tips outlined above, you can take control of your credit and set yourself up for financial success in the long term.

Derogatory Marks

Derogatory marks, also known as negative items, are items that can appear on your credit report and have a negative impact on your credit score. Examples of derogatory marks include late payments, collections, bankruptcies, foreclosures, and charge-offs. These marks can remain on your credit report for several years and can make it more difficult to get approved for credit or loans. Here, we'll explore what derogatory marks are, how they can impact your credit score, and some tips for maintaining a good credit score in spite of derogatory marks.

First, let's define what derogatory marks are. Derogatory marks are negative items that can appear on your credit report and have a negative impact on your credit score. They can include:

1. **Late payments**: Late payments occur when you fail to pay your bills on time. They can have a significant impact on your credit score, especially if you have a pattern of consistently making late payments.
2. **Collections**: Collections occur when a creditor turns your unpaid debt over to a collection agency. Collections can have a severe impact on your credit score and can remain on your credit report for seven years.
3. **Bankruptcies**: Bankruptcy is a legal process in which you can discharge some or all of your debts. While bankruptcy can provide relief from overwhelming debt, it can also have a severe impact on your credit score and can remain on your credit report for up to 10 years.
4. **Foreclosures**: Foreclosure is a process in which a lender takes possession of your home because you defaulted on your mortgage. Foreclosure can have a severe impact on your credit score and can remain on your credit report for up to seven years.
5. **Charge-offs**: Charge-offs occur when a creditor writes off your debt as a loss because you have not paid it for an extended period of time. Charge-offs can have a significant impact on your credit score and can remain on your credit report for up to seven years.

Now that we've defined derogatory marks, let's talk about how they can impact your credit score:

1. **They can lower your credit score**: Derogatory marks can have a significant impact on your credit score because they signal to lenders and creditors that you have a history of financial instability or irresponsible credit use. The more derogatory marks you have, the lower your credit score will be.
2. **They can make it more difficult to get approved for credit**: Derogatory marks can make it more difficult to get approved for credit or loans because they signal to lenders and creditors that you may be a high-risk borrower. You may be more likely to get approved for credit with more favorable terms if you have a good credit score and few or no derogatory marks.

Now that we've discussed what derogatory marks are and how they can impact your credit score, let's go over some tips for maintaining a good credit score in spite of derogatory marks:

1. **Pay your bills on time**: One of the best ways to maintain a good credit score is to pay your bills on time. Late payments can have a significant impact on your credit score, so it's important to make sure you pay your bills on time every month.
2. **Dispute errors on your credit report**: If you notice errors on your credit report, such as derogatory marks that you don't believe are accurate, you can dispute them with the credit bureaus. The credit bureaus are required to investigate your dispute and correct any errors on your credit report.
3. **Pay off collections**: If you have collections on your credit report, try to pay them off as soon as possible. While paying off a collection won't remove it from your credit report, it can improve your credit score and make it easier to get approved for credit in the future.
4. **Seek credit counseling**: If you are struggling with debt or financial instability, credit counseling can help you get back on track. Credit counseling agencies can help you develop a budget, negotiate with creditors, and create a debt repayment plan.
5. **Be patient**: Building or rebuilding your credit takes time, so it's important to be patient and stay committed to improving your credit score. It can take several months or even years to see significant improvement in your credit score, but by using credit responsibly and paying your bills on time, you can improve your credit score over time.

In conclusion, derogatory marks are negative items that can appear on your credit report and have a negative impact on your credit score. They can include late payments, collections, bankruptcies, foreclosures, and charge-offs. Derogatory marks can make it more difficult to get approved for credit and can result in higher interest rates, but by paying your bills on time, disputing errors on your credit report, and seeking credit counseling if needed, you can maintain a good credit score in spite of derogatory marks. It's important to be patient and stay committed to improving your credit score, as it can take time to see significant improvement.

Hard Inquiries

Hard inquiries, also known as credit checks, are credit checks that are initiated by lenders or creditors when you apply for credit, such as a credit card or loan. Hard inquiries can have a temporary negative impact on your credit score because they signal to lenders and creditors that you are seeking new credit. Here, we'll explore what hard inquiries are, how they can affect your credit score, and some tips for maintaining a good credit score in spite of hard inquiries.

First, let's define what hard inquiries are. Hard inquiries are credit checks that are initiated by lenders or creditors when you apply for credit. They are called "hard" inquiries because they can have a temporary negative impact on your credit score. Examples of hard inquiries include applying for a credit card, mortgage, car loan, or personal loan.

Now that we've defined hard inquiries, let's talk about how they can affect your credit score:

1. **They can lower your credit score**: Hard inquiries can have a temporary negative impact on your credit score because they signal to lenders and creditors that you are seeking new credit. The more hard inquiries you have, the lower your credit score will be.
2. **They can make it more difficult to get approved for credit**: Hard inquiries can make it more difficult to get approved for credit or loans because they signal to lenders and creditors that you are seeking new credit. You may be more likely to get approved for credit with more favorable terms if you have a good credit score and few or no hard inquiries.

Now that we've discussed what hard inquiries are and how they can affect your credit score, let's go over some tips for maintaining a good credit score in spite of hard inquiries:

1. **Shop around for credit**: If you are in the market for a credit card or loan, it's a good idea to shop around and compare offers from different lenders. This can help you find the best deal and minimize the number of hard inquiries on your credit report.

2. **Don't apply for credit unnecessarily**: It's important to only apply for credit when you really need it. Avoid applying for credit unnecessarily, as this can result in unnecessary hard inquiries on your credit report.
3. **Pay your bills on time**: One of the best ways to maintain a good credit score is to pay your bills on time. Late payments can have a significant impact on your credit score, so it's important to make sure you pay your bills on time every month.
4. **Dispute errors on your credit report**: If you notice errors on your credit report, such as hard inquiries that you don't believe are accurate, you can dispute them with the credit bureaus. The credit bureaus are required to investigate your dispute and correct any errors on your credit report.
5. **Be patient**: Building or rebuilding your credit takes time, so it's important to be patient and stay committed to improving your credit score. It can take several months or even years to see significant improvement in your credit score, but by using credit responsibly and paying your bills on time, you can improve your credit score over time.

In conclusion, hard inquiries are credit checks that are initiated by lenders or creditors when you apply for credit. They can have a temporary negative impact on your credit score because they signal to lenders and creditors that you are seeking new credit. To maintain a good credit score in spite of hard inquiries, it's important to shop around for credit, avoid applying for credit unnecessarily, pay your bills on time, dispute errors on your credit report, and be patient. By following these tips, you can take control of your credit and set yourself up for financial success in the long term.

Credit-Repair Services

If you have negative items on your credit report, such as late payments, collections, or bankruptcies, you may be considering hiring a credit-repair agency to help fix your credit. Credit-repair agencies offer a variety of services to help you improve your credit score and get back on track financially. Here, we'll explore the different types of services credit-repair agencies offer and explain exactly how they provide these services. We'll also discuss the typical costs associated with credit-repair services.

First, let's define what credit-repair agencies are. Credit-repair agencies are companies that help individuals improve their credit scores by disputing errors on their credit reports and negotiating with creditors to remove negative items. Credit-repair agencies are regulated by the Credit Repair Organizations Act (CROA), which requires them to disclose their fees and services clearly and prohibits them from making false or misleading statements.

Credit-repair companies offer a variety of services to help individuals improve their credit scores and financial standing. These services can include:

1. **Reviewing credit reports**: Credit-repair companies typically start by reviewing an individual's credit reports from the three major credit bureaus (Experian, Equifax, and TransUnion). They look for errors or inaccuracies that may be negatively impacting an individual's credit score, such as incorrect personal information, incorrect account information, or accounts that have been wrongly reported as delinquent.
2. **Dispute resolution**: Credit-repair companies can help individuals dispute errors or inaccuracies on their credit reports. This can involve working with the credit bureaus to have incorrect information removed or corrected, or working with creditors to resolve disputes over outstanding debts.
3. **Credit counseling**: Credit-repair companies may offer credit counseling services to help individuals better understand their credit scores and how to improve them. This can include providing education on credit management, budgeting, and financial planning.

4. **Debt negotiation**: Some credit-repair companies offer debt negotiation services, which involve working with creditors to reduce the amount of debt owed or to negotiate more favorable terms for repayment. This can include negotiating lower interest rates or longer repayment periods.
5. **Credit-building assistance**: Credit-repair companies may also offer assistance in building credit, such as by helping individuals obtain secured credit cards or loans to establish a credit history.
6. **Identity theft protection**: Some credit-repair companies offer identity theft protection services, which can include monitoring credit reports for signs of identity theft and helping individuals recover from identity theft if it occurs.

It's important to note that credit-repair companies are not able to remove accurate and verifiable information from an individual's credit reports. They can only work to have incorrect or outdated information removed or corrected. Additionally, credit-repair services can be expensive, and it's important to carefully research any company before signing up for their services. It may be more cost-effective to try to improve your credit on your own, by paying your bills on time, keeping your credit utilization low, and avoiding taking on too much debt.

Now that we've discussed the different types of services credit-repair agencies offer, let's talk about how they provide these services:

1. **Credit report dispute services**: Credit-repair agencies typically start by reviewing your credit report and identifying any errors or negative items that may be affecting your credit score. They will then contact the credit bureaus and creditors on your behalf to dispute these errors and request that they be removed from your credit report.
2. **Debt settlement services**: Credit-repair agencies may negotiate with your creditors to remove negative items from your credit report in exchange for payment. They may also help you negotiate a lower interest rate or payment plan to make it easier for you to pay off your debts.
3. **Credit counseling services**: Credit-repair agencies may provide credit counseling services to help you develop a budget, negotiate with creditors, and create a debt repayment plan. They may also provide resources, such as educational materials and financial tools,

to help you understand how credit works and how to use credit responsibly.
4. **Credit education services**: Credit-repair agencies may provide educational resources, such as credit repair guides, credit score calculators, and credit score simulators, to help you understand how credit works and how to use credit responsibly.

Now that we've discussed the different types of services credit-repair agencies offer and how they provide these services, let's talk about the typical costs associated with credit-repair services:

1. Credit-repair agencies typically charge a fee for their services. The cost of credit-repair services can vary significantly, depending on the complexity of your credit situation and the services you need. Some credit-repair agencies charge a flat fee for their services, while others charge a monthly fee.
2. Credit-repair agencies may also charge additional fees for specific services, such as credit report dispute services or debt settlement services. These fees may be charged on a per-item basis or as a percentage of the amount of debt being negotiated.
3. Credit-repair agencies are required by law to disclose their fees and services clearly, so it's important to ask about all fees upfront and to carefully review any contracts or agreements before signing.

In conclusion, credit-repair agencies offer a variety of services to help individuals improve their credit scores, including credit report dispute services, debt settlement services, credit counseling services, and credit education services. Credit-repair agencies typically charge a fee for their services, which can vary significantly depending on the complexity of your credit situation and the services you need. It's important to carefully research credit-repair agencies and to ask about all fees upfront before signing any contracts or agreements.

Utilizing Your Credit

Having a good credit score is essential for your financial well-being. A good credit score can help you save money on interest, get approved for credit and loans, and even improve your job prospects. In this article, we'll explore the benefits of having a good credit score, how it can help you save money, and how you can utilize your credit to make more money.

First, let's define what a credit score is. A credit score is a three-digit number that reflects your creditworthiness, or how likely you are to pay back your debts. Credit scores are based on the information in your credit report, which is a detailed record of your credit history. Your credit report includes information about your credit accounts, such as credit cards, mortgages, and loans, as well as your payment history and credit utilization. Credit scores typically range from 300 to 850, with higher scores indicating a lower risk of default.

Now that we've defined credit scores, let's talk about the benefits of having a good credit score:

1. **Save money on interest**: One of the primary benefits of having a good credit score is that it can help you save money on interest. Lenders and creditors use your credit score to determine the risk of lending you money, and they typically offer lower interest rates to borrowers with good credit scores. By having a good credit score, you may be able to qualify for lower interest rates on credit cards, mortgages, and loans, which can save you thousands of dollars in interest over time.
2. **Get approved for credit and loans**: Another benefit of having a good credit score is that it can make it easier to get approved for credit and loans. Lenders and creditors are more likely to approve your applications for credit and loans if you have a good credit score, and you may also be able to qualify for more favorable terms, such as lower interest rates or higher credit limits.
3. **Improve your job prospects**: Having a good credit score can also improve your job prospects. Many employers check the credit scores of job candidates, especially for positions that involve handling money or managing sensitive financial information. A good credit score can

demonstrate to an employer that you are responsible and trustworthy, which can make you a more attractive job candidate.

Now that we've discussed the benefits of having a good credit score, let's talk about how it can help you save money:

1. **Lower interest rates**: As mentioned previously, having a good credit score can qualify you for lower interest rates on credit cards, mortgages, and loans. This can save you money on interest charges and make it easier to pay off your debts.
2. **Lower insurance premiums**: Your credit score can also affect your insurance premiums. Many insurance companies use credit scores as a factor in determining your insurance rates, and you may be able to qualify for lower premiums if you have a good credit score.
3. **Avoid fees**: Having a good credit score can also help you avoid fees, such as late payment fees and overdraft fees. By paying your bills on time and maintaining a good credit score, you can avoid these fees and save money.

Now that we've discussed how having a good credit score can help you save money, let's talk about how you can utilize your credit to make more money:

1. **Invest in real estate**: If you have a good credit score and a solid financial foundation, you may be able to use your credit to invest in real estate. You can use your credit to buy rental properties or to flip houses, which can generate passive income and increase your net worth over time.
2. **Start a business**: Another way you can utilize your credit to make more money is by starting a business. You can use your credit to finance your business, whether it's a small online store or a brick-and-mortar storefront. By having a good credit score, you may be able to qualify for business loans or credit cards with favorable terms, which can help you get your business off the ground.
3. **Invest in stocks**: If you have a good credit score and a solid financial foundation, you may also be able to use your credit to invest in stocks. You can use a margin account, which allows you to borrow money from your brokerage firm to buy stocks, or you can use a credit card to make investments. This can be a risky strategy, but if

you do your research and invest wisely, you may be able to make more money through stock investments.

In conclusion, having a good credit score has many benefits, including saving money on interest, getting approved for credit and loans, and improving your job prospects. A good credit score can also help you save money by qualifying you for lower insurance premiums and helping you avoid fees. You can also utilize your credit to make more money by investing in real estate, starting a business, or investing in stocks. By understanding the importance of your credit score and using credit responsibly, you can set yourself up for financial success in the long term.

Platforms to view your credit

Your credit score and credit report are important tools that can help you understand your financial health and make informed decisions about credit and loans. There are several platforms available that allow you to view your credit score and credit report, each with its own unique features and benefits. Here, we'll explore the different types of platforms to view your credit score and credit report, and discuss the pros and cons of each.

1. **Credit bureaus**: The three major credit bureaus – Experian, Equifax, and TransUnion – are the primary sources for credit scores and credit reports. You can request a copy of your credit report from each credit bureau once per year for free through AnnualCreditReport.com. You can also request a copy of your credit report for a fee if you need it more frequently or if you have been denied credit or insurance.

Pros: Credit bureaus offer detailed credit reports that include information about your credit accounts, payment history, and credit utilization. You can use this information to understand your credit history and identify areas for improvement. Credit bureaus also offer a range of credit-related products and services, such as credit monitoring and identity theft protection, for a fee.

Cons: Credit bureaus may charge a fee for access to your credit report or credit-related products and services. Additionally, your credit report from each credit bureau may not be identical, as they may receive different information from lenders and creditors.

2. **Credit card issuers**: Many credit card issuers offer free access to your credit score and credit report as a benefit to cardholders. You can typically view your credit score and credit report through your credit card issuer's online portal or mobile app

3. **Credit score websites**: There are several websites that offer free access to your credit score, such as Credit Karma, Credit Sesame, and NerdWallet. These websites typically use data from one or more of the credit bureaus to provide your credit score and credit report.

Pros: Credit score websites offer free access to your credit score and credit report, as well as educational resources and tools to help you understand your credit and make informed financial decisions. Many credit score websites also offer credit monitoring and alerts, which can help you identify and address potential credit issues.

Cons: Credit score websites may not use data from all three credit bureaus, so your credit score and credit report may not be complete or accurate. Additionally, credit score websites may have a financial interest in the products and services they recommend, so it's important to compare offers and shop around.

4. **Mobile apps**: There are several mobile apps that offer access to your credit score and credit report, such as CreditWise from Capital One and Credit Scorecard from Discover. These apps typically use data from one or more of the credit bureaus to provide your credit score and credit report.

Pros: Mobile apps offer convenient access to your credit score and credit report from your smartphone or tablet. Many mobile apps also offer credit monitoring and alerts, as well as educational resources and tools to help you understand your credit.

Cons: Mobile apps may not use data from all three credit bureaus, so your credit score and credit report may not be complete or accurate. Additionally, mobile apps may have a financial interest in the products and services they recommend, so it's important to compare offers and shop around.

In conclusion, there are several platforms available to view your credit score and credit report, including credit bureaus, credit card issuers, credit score websites, and mobile apps. Each platform has its own unique features and benefits, and it's important to choose the platform that best meets your needs and budget. Regardless of which platform you choose, it's important to review your credit score and credit report regularly to ensure accuracy and identify areas for improvement.

Goodbye

Dear reader,

Thank you for joining us on this journey to repair and improve your credit. We hope that the information and guidance we provided in this book has been helpful to you, and that you feel more confident and empowered to take control of your financial future.

We understand that credit repair is not a one-time event, but rather a continuous process that requires patience and discipline. We encourage you to continue to monitor your credit and make informed financial decisions that will help you maintain a good credit score.

If you have any questions or need further guidance, we encourage you to seek out the resources and support you need to succeed. There are many organizations and professionals who can help you understand your credit and make informed financial decisions.

As we conclude this book, we want to thank you for your attention and commitment to improving your credit. We hope that you have gained valuable insights and skills that will help you achieve your financial goals.

Wishing you the best of luck on your credit repair journey.

Sincerely, Rodrigo Carbonell

www.ingramcontent.com/pod-product-compliance
Lightning Source LLC
Chambersburg PA
CBHW050327220526
45465CB00005B/2163